I'm Going to Be a Little Brother?

Written by Amanda Giardinelli
Illustrated by Danielle Early

First Edition

Published by Kate Butler Books
www.katebutlerbooks.com

ISBN: 978-1-952725-63-0

To my husband, Brian,
my parents,
and my sister, Taylor.
Thank you for always supporting me
throughout life's many adventures.

To the children that I nanny,
Julia, Tyler and Lilly.
We have grown up alongside of each other throughout the years.
Thank you for giving me the idea for my first book.
To Andy and Sarah, thank you for allowing me
to be a part of your family.

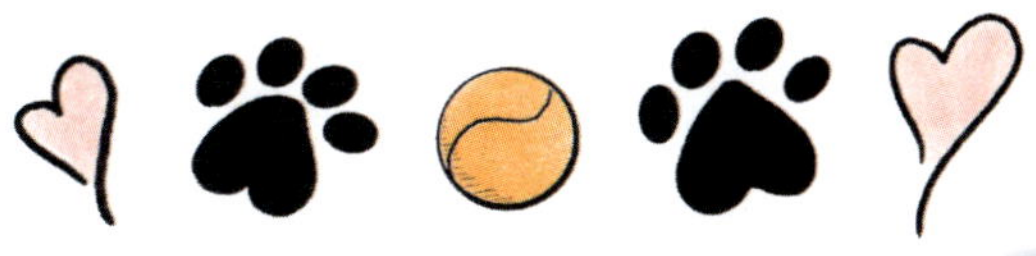

"Hi, I'm Rommel!"

"Mom and Dad are getting me a sister! I'm so excited! I've always wanted to be a big brother!"

"I'll teach her how to play fetch. I love when Mom throws my favorite ball!"

“I’ll teach her how to play tug-of-war. It’s my favorite game to play with Dad!”

"I'll teach her how to give LOTS of kisses! Mom and Dad love kisses!"

"Mom and Dad are taking me to meet my sister. Her name is Jamie."

Rommel is confused when he meets Jamie. Jamie isn't a puppy, which Rommel was expecting. Jamie is taller, and older than he is.

"Does this mean
I'm going to be a
little brother?"

Jamie is quiet and shy, and doesn't want to play.

"Mom and Dad tell me to be patient with Jamie, and to keep showing her kindness because she is scared of her new home."

"Jamie used to live with another family, but her dad got really sick," Rommel says. "Mom and Dad adopted Jamie into our family so that she will always having a loving home."

“Jamie and I will become best friends,” Rommel thought. “I’m going to be the best *little* brother!”

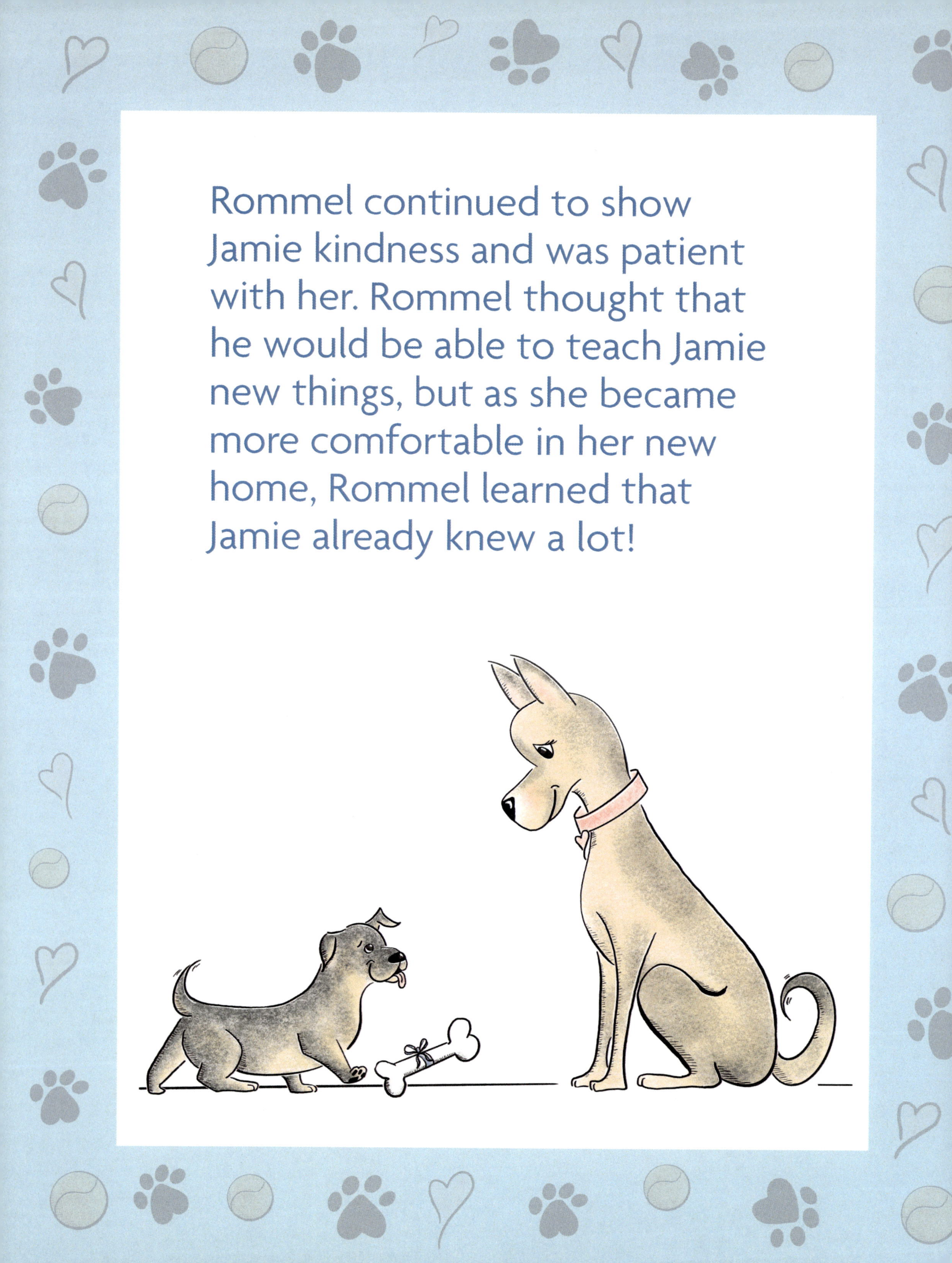

Rommel continued to show Jamie kindness and was patient with her. Rommel thought that he would be able to teach Jamie new things, but as she became more comfortable in her new home, Rommel learned that Jamie already knew a lot!

"Jamie loves to play fetch,"
Rommel says.

"We love to race after the ball! Jamie is so fast and can jump high in the air to catch the ball."

“Jamie loves to play tug-of-war,”
Rommel says. “She’s so strong!”

"Jamie also loves to give LOTS of kisses!"

"Thank you for helping me," Jamie says.

"How did I help you?" Rommel asks. "I didn't teach you how to play fetch, or how to play tug-of-war."

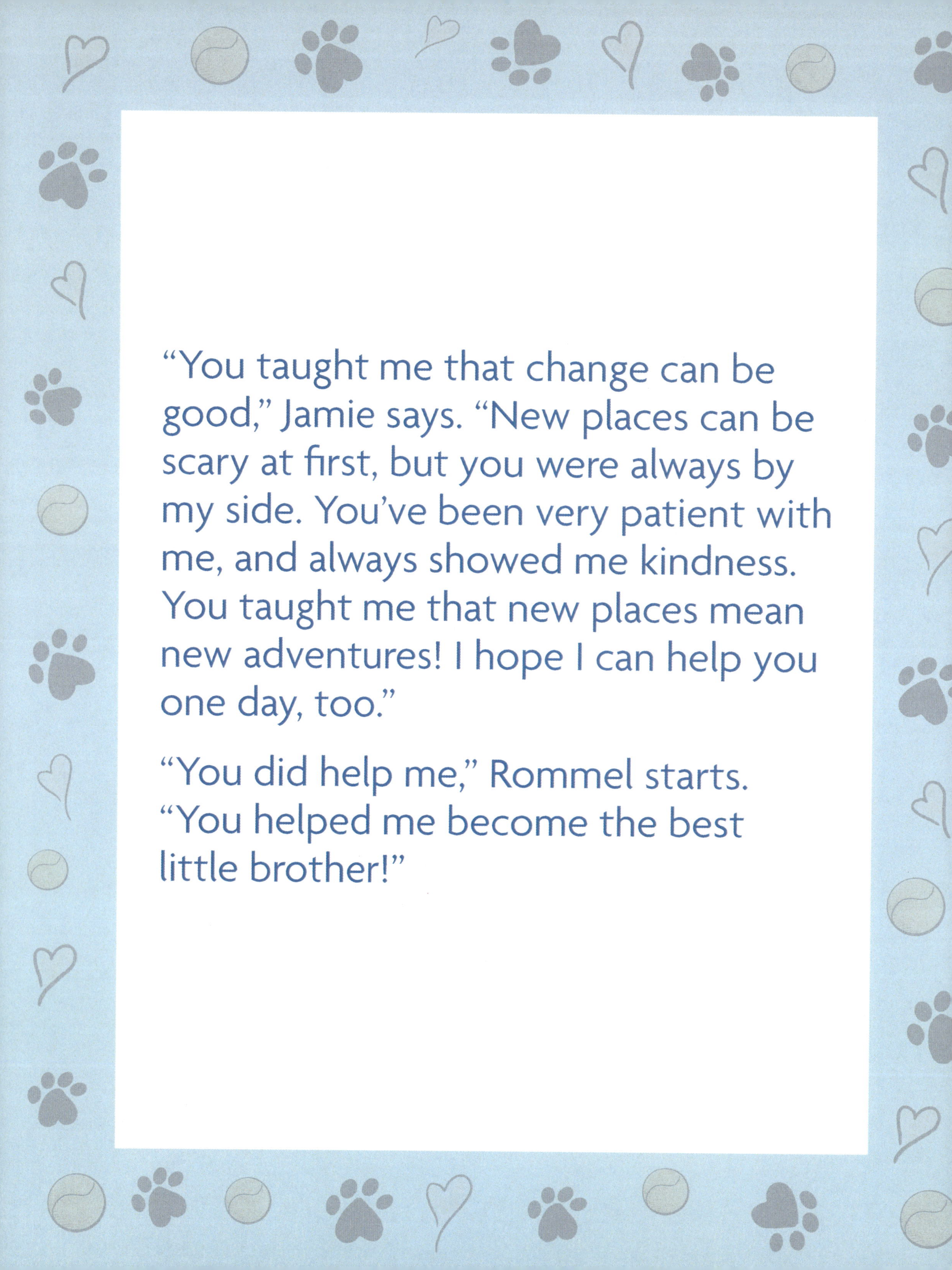

"You taught me that change can be good," Jamie says. "New places can be scary at first, but you were always by my side. You've been very patient with me, and always showed me kindness. You taught me that new places mean new adventures! I hope I can help you one day, too."

"You did help me," Rommel starts. "You helped me become the best little brother!"

Love,
Rommel & Jamie

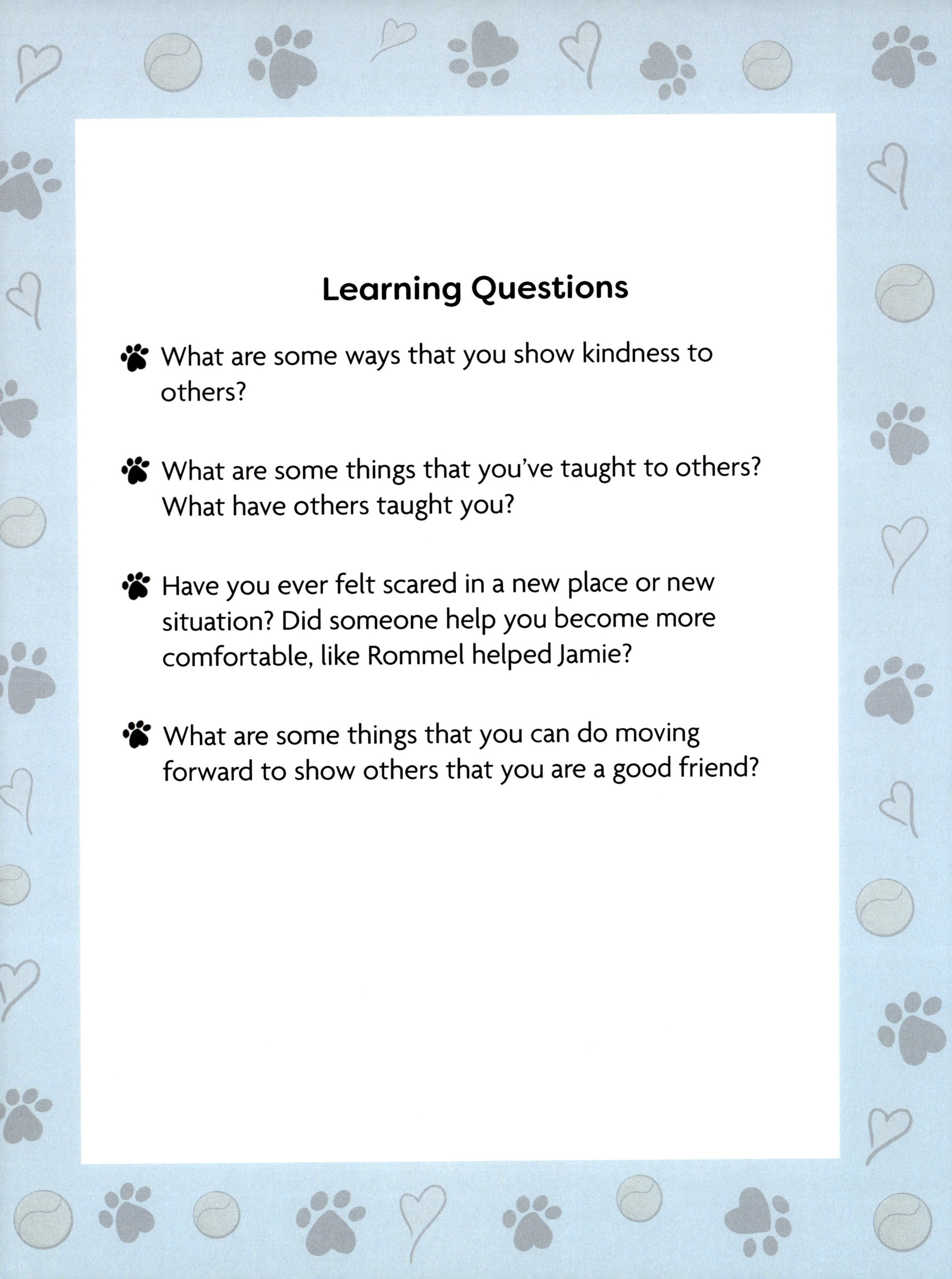

Learning Questions

- What are some ways that you show kindness to others?
- What are some things that you've taught to others? What have others taught you?
- Have you ever felt scared in a new place or new situation? Did someone help you become more comfortable, like Rommel helped Jamie?
- What are some things that you can do moving forward to show others that you are a good friend?

About the Author

Amanda lives in Pennsylvania with her husband, Brian, their two German Shepherds, Rommel and Jamie, and their three cats. Amanda is a nurse, and has been a nanny for a family of three children since 2014. Soon after bringing Rommel home in January of 2017, Amanda and Brian knew that he needed a sibling/friend. In August of 2018, Amanda and Brian were introduced to a gentleman who was looking for a loving home for Jamie, as he had been diagnosed with a rare form of cancer and wanted to make sure that Jamie would always be cared for and loved. After battling cancer herself, and losing Brian's father after a long fight with cancer, Amanda felt as though meeting Jamie was meant to be. Jamie was overcoming depression and anxiety, as she had previously worked as a Search and Rescue K9. Amanda and Brian were amazed and inspired by Rommel's gentle heart and kind spirit, as he helped Jamie become more comfortable in her new home. Rommel and Jamie are now inseparable!

Made in the USA
Middletown, DE
09 June 2021

41650156R00015